THE DADDY
ANIMAL BOOK

Also by Jennifer Cossins

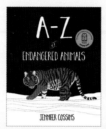
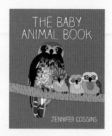

THE DADDY ANIMAL BOOK

Jennifer Cossins

LOTHIAN
Children's Books

A daddy polar bear is called a boar.
A baby polar bear is called a cub.

A boar can be as heavy as a car,
but its cubs are born no heavier
than a jar of honey.

A **daddy zebra** is called a **stallion**.
A **baby zebra** is called a **foal**.

A foal can run to its dad
just one hour after being born.

A **daddy turkey** is called a **gobbler**.
A **baby turkey** is called a **poult**.

A poult learns how to fly when it is only two weeks old, and grows up to be a fast runner and high jumper too.

A **daddy sheep** is called a **ram**.
A **baby sheep** is called a **lamb**.

A ram's horns are made of the
same stuff as your fingernails.

A daddy penguin is called a cock.
A baby penguin is called a chick.

While his mate looks for food, an Emperor cock balances their egg on his toes, warm and safe next to his tummy and well away from the ice.

A **daddy duck** is called a **drake**.
A **baby duck** is called a **duckling**.

A duckling is only ten hours old
when it goes for its very first swim.

A **daddy ferret** is called a **hob**.
A **baby ferret** is called a **kit**.

A newborn kit can't see or
hear yet, and spends most of
its time deeply asleep.

A daddy hippopotamus is called a bull.
A baby hippopotamus is called a calf.

To protect his family and home
from danger, a bull opens his
mouth wide and bellows loudly.

A **daddy wombat** is called a jack.
A **baby wombat** is called a joey.

A wombat joey is about the size
of a jellybean when it's born.

A **daddy goose** is called a **gander**.
A **baby goose** is called a **gosling**.

A gander closely guards his mate's nest, keeping their eggs safe until the goslings hatch.

A **daddy cougar** is called a lion.
A **baby cougar** is called a **kitten**.

A kitten is born with lots of spots,
but these slowly fade until its fur
is all one colour like its dad's.

A daddy eagle is called a tiercel.
A baby eagle is called an eaglet.

A tiercel and his mate build an
enormous nest together that
they use year after year for
all their eaglets.

A **daddy mouse** is called a **buck**.
A **baby mouse** is called a **pinkie**.

A newborn pinkie is pink and
hairless, but grows all its fur
in only ten days.

A **daddy gorilla** is called a **silverback**.
A **baby gorilla** is called an **infant**.

Silverbacks and infants love
playing games and spending
time together.

A Lothian Children's Book

Published in Australia and New Zealand in 2020
by Hachette Australia
Level 17, 207 Kent Street, Sydney NSW 2000
www.hachettechildrens.com.au

1 3 5 7 9 10 8 6 4 2

Text and illustration copyright © Jennifer Cossins 2020

 A catalogue record for this
book is available from the
National Library of Australia

ISBN 978 0 7344 1987 3 (hardback)

Designed by Kinart
Colour reproduction by Splitting Image
Printed in China by Toppan Leefung Printing Limited